WHAT PEOPLE ARE SAYING ABOUT.

Transcending Personal Apocalypse

"If ever you have experienced a dark night of the soul – when the bottom drops out and you and your reality fall apart and you eventually hit rock bottom without hope or any sense of how to carry on – then this book is for you. How good it would be in times like these to have a caring and compassionate friend to accompany you. One who understands what you're going through, has been there themselves, and can help you find your way out. In Transcending Personal Apocalypse: Replace Your Beliefs, Revitalize Your Future, Douglas Breitbart and Fabian Szulanski show up in precisely this role. Rather than offer quick fix remedies or feel-good solutions, they lead you on an empowering exploration of self-inquiry. "Each of us is the creator of our life," they affirm, so they offer a journey that is "about replacing low-level but pervasive fear, with a profound sense of wellbeing; and a shift … to curiosity and excitement about what the future has in store." In short, it is a book about unstuckedness through "a process of self-inquiry, in service to provide a clean slate upon which a new life story can be written." I also share this quote from George Bernard Shaw which came to mind as I read your book: "Imagination is the beginning of creation. You imagine what you desire, you will what you imagine and at last you create what you will."

Alexander Laszlo, Ph.D.
President
Bertalanffy Center
for the Study of Systems Science

"Unlike other books, Breitbart and Szulanski do not attempt to give the magic recipe to change our lives by telling us how to do it in a simplistic way. The proposal is to accompany us in the search for disruptive episodes in personal history (AP) that could condition us in the choices and behavior patterns that today limit us and prevent us from living our lives with a personal, unique sense, according to our potentialities. and real possibilities.

From this perspective, they emphasize "being" and the search for genuine identity (who am I?) Rather than automatic "doing" that compulsively repeats frustrations and failures. Interesting proposal in the current contexts of uncertainty and social anguish, in which diving into our interior and building a new autobiography becomes a precious and essential asset. The authors, in this sense, successfully motivate us for this deep exploration prior to action. Let's accept the challenge. Congratulations!"

Martín Yechúa
Executive Director
Asociación de Directorios Asociados

"Doug and Fabián have put words to the subconscious struggle that is life for so many of us. This eternal wisdom can bring transcendent light to even the darkest of personal apocalypses."

Hayden Smith
Transformation Lead
Siemens Energy

"Reader beware! This book is NOT written in the typical style of a self-help book. It bypasses all the old ways of working with trauma and goes straight to what lies at the heart of everything, YOU!

This book supports you to take a different look at life and most of all how you respond to what life has given you. This book is not an easy read. It will keep you on your toes, it will trip you up, it will make you want to burn it, yet most of all it will be there to help you gain your center and empower you in a way that is unique to you. Only you can bring you back to the authentic being you are. This book guides and empowers you to take your power back."

Will Van Inwagen
Co-Founder
Being In Systems LLC
Founder: Enlivening Edge Community Conversations

"You ask, "Have I felt a life changing event... like the world has disappeared under my feet? Am I scared, anxious, tense, uncertain... unable to make sense or identify the way forward?"

OMG...how did you know? (You did know right?) This terrible virus and the total economic shutdown absolutely made my world disappear. I am scared and I can't really see the way forward. And I'm sure that's true for most of us.

Two choices in what to do. Either, we can hope that someone else will make things okay again or we can do it ourselves, for ourselves, our loved ones, and for our communities. I'm choosing the second; Do it myself for myself and my loved ones!

And to tell me how, along comes your great work, "Transcending Personal Apocalypse - Replace your Beliefs, Revitalize your Future." What you've created is a roadmap for transcending this monumental coronavirus challenge.

It's thorough and honest and relevant; and filled with good ideas and spot on insights. No! It's clear we're not going to go back to business as usual. To revitalize the future we need to replace a lot and make big changes. Thank you for explaining how to get started."

Laurence Haughton
Head of R&D
Jason Jennings
Co-Author: *The Highspeed Company*

"I can't imagine anyone going through life without a few personal apocalypses. Personally I've had quite a few, and this is the book I wish I'd read before the first one. If I had, it wouldn't have taken me so many personal apocalypses to figure this out.

If you've had one, read it to prepare for the next one. If you're having one now, read it to get out of it. And if you haven't had one, then read it before you do. Life is about trial and learning, and the learning here is likely to serve you well, now and into the future."

Gene Bellinger
Founder
System Thinking World
Author: *Beyond Connecting the Dots*

"From a very motivating title, the authors reflect on "Personal Apocalypse" (PA), as a life event that is experienced as personally devastating. Who has not had a PA in his own life? The book inspires deep reflections from personal knowledge, without cases or recipes.

There are many experiences and signals that serve to highlight our path of transformation, after the impact of a PA situation.

I find this book both stimulating and a powerful read."

José Luis Roces
Past Executive President
Instituto Tecnológico de Buenos Aires
Author: *El Líder Vital*

"First you should know I love what you guys have written. As a 73-year-old who has managed a print company for 30 years and taught designers for 10, I have had a couple of serious traumas in my life. I speak as someone who knows it. I wish I had this book 20 years ago."

Michael Josefowicz
Founder
Center for Global Study of
Social Enterprise
Creator: The PrinterNet Project

"This book arrives at a most appropriate time. Every single one of us needs to master the art of transcending the unpredictable, especially in the times that we are living. The master key to the door of freedom lies with understanding how to break free from the chains of automatic thinking when faced with a life- changing event. This book offers a practical roadmap for doing just that."

Juan Matías Fernandez Larghi
Executive Director
Inversora Altue
Author: *Acción*

"Transcending Personal Apocalypse" is a compelling read and I read it in one go. I found the book an easy read, although the underlying request requires your participation and sometimes the support of a professional.

This book takes the mystery out of these life changing events and opens you up to smorgasbords of choices. I was reminded of the many phases I have gone through during my life and how I could not help nodding away and as I read it."

Amaranatho Maurice Roby
Founder
Mindfulness out of the box
Creator: The PlayfulMonk Programs

"For anyone who has experienced a traumatic event such as job loss, major illness, divorce or even a challenging situation, Transcending Personal Apocalypse is a must read. It takes you on a powerful journey of reflection and insight into the issues both personal and societal, which are at the heart of these painful yet ultimately transformative situations.

Describing ways to separate the oftentimes overwhelming emotional energy from the experience itself, this book helps you to begin to work with and perceive these situations from a place of clarity, reconnecting you with your inner power and potential. Very inspiring!"

Sharron Rose
President
Sacred Mysteries Productions
Author: *The Path of the Priestess*

"I'm particularly touched by the compassion expressed behind the lines in this book. This is a precious gift for many people living in a VUCA (volatile, uncertain, complex and ambiguous) world. I've had my personal apocalypse, and I'm sure we all have or will have a personal apocalypse.

What's fascinating about this book, I feel, is the clear and clean messages from an emergent and generative place. It is showing us a path to connect with our inner wisdom and recognize: we always have a choice and we're the source of light and wisdom."

Chunfeng "Breeze" Dong
Global Leadership
Learning Program Manager
ABB Switzerland AG

"Well, here we are just entering a global crisis of huge magnitude and a great many of us are now suffering deeply through both the personal and collective apocalypse (Covid-19, that is), and with perfect timing along come Douglas and Fabian with some very welcome words of wisdom to guide us as we seek a firmed foundation of personal strength and surety.

This will surely help us to keep our balance as we navigate the turbulent time we are entering. The advice in this book is thus highly relevant and reassuring. Read this book, take it to heart, and put it into practice as well."

Langdon Morris
CEO
Innovation Labs
Author: *The Big Shift*

TRANSCENDING PERSONAL APOCALYPSE

Replace Your Beliefs, Revitalize Your Future

Douglas Breitbart, Fabián Szulanski

THE
VALUES
FOUNDATION PRESS

TRANSCENDING PERSONAL APOCALYPSE

First Edition
Published June 24, 2021
Douglas Breitbart & Fabián Szulanski
TheValuesFoundation.org
+1 551 804 7251

THE
VALUES
FOUNDATION PRESS

Bridgman, Michigan, USA
June, 2021

ISBN: 978-1-7351576-2-7

Table of Contents

ACKNOWLEDGEMENTS

We would like to thank all of the people without whose assistance this book might not have been written.

Firstly, to our life partners, who have always been there for us in our individual journeys; and provided the faith, belief and emotional support through our own life experiences, Andreína Sayag and Cheryl Breitbart—thank you!

Secondly, to the brilliant authors responsible for the books listed in our Appendix. They have provided critical pieces of the human puzzle. Their work has provided clarity, and proved essential for each of us on a personal level, along with millions of other devoted readers.

Lastly, to those who put shoulder to the wheel and generously assisted with their feedback, comments, criticisms, proofreading, and editing talents: Anna Harris, Amaranatho Maurice Robey, Michael Josefowicz, Dave Wolf, Tammy Lea Meyer, Harry van de Velde, Gene Bellinger, Barry Kort, Lori Sortino, Rachel Aharon-Eini, Will Van Inwagen, Brenda Bitman, Jorge Feldman, Alejandro Poleri, and Juan Matías Fernández Larghi, Chunfeng "Breeze" Dong, Langdon Morris, Alexander Laszlo, Sharron Rose, Hayden Smith, Martín Yechúa, Laurence Haughton, and José Luis Roces.

PROLOGUE

As proud baby boomers, hailing from two different continents, with a handful of hats and careers under each of our respective belts; we have found ourselves and many of our friends, colleagues, and acquaintances sharing a common experience.

That experience is being confronted with a profound life-disrupting event; and recovery from it being elusive despite one's best efforts to do so.

We have coined the term *Personal Apocalypse* ("PA") to describe a life event that is experienced as personally devastating and catastrophic. That impact is often invisible to others around us.

We see many struggling with the aftermath of these PA events in their lives today. The effects can be emotional, physical, spiritual, cognitive, behavioral, circumstantial, and sensorial.

In exploring the impacts of PAs, the person affected can be fully engaged and proactive in addressing what has happened; and yet their best efforts and attempts to recover persistently fail.

We have sought to unpack: the most common events; the experiential impacts on individual awareness and effectiveness; and the root causes of the chronic frustration that can arise from failing to achieve the desired result.

We have also sought to feel into and share our take on these experiences from the inside out, from a reader's perspective of being stuck in a post-PA life.

Our goal is to help those wrestling with post-PA challenges to make sense of their life and unique circumstances, and unpack and reframe their path forward.

This book is not intended as a prescriptive checklist or recipe for how to recover from PA events. What is shared is based on our and others' discoveries about the "why" behind what may not be working in one's life, in the wake of a PA.

As we peel the onion, we recognize that any one layer may or may not resonate. However, we hope that you may find valuable takeaways that serve as a doorway through which a new awareness can emerge.

Have You Experienced a PA?

Have you experienced a significant life event, either within or outside of your control, that has left you feeling as if the world has dissolved from under your feet? Has the impact of this experience left you without any familiar landmarks or means to cope with your new reality in a sustainable way?

Have you or are you experiencing feelings of being lost, powerless, anxious, or afraid; with a frustrating inability to make sense or see a path forward?

Have you found yourself repeatedly returning to the same strategies or solutions that have proven to be ineffective, in the hope that this time it will work?

If you have answered yes to any or all of the above, then it is highly likely you may have experienced a PA event.

What is a Personal Apocalypse?

Many of us experience times or events in our lives when all that we know and believe vanishes before our eyes. This can be sudden, as with a personal health crisis or automobile accident, or over time, as with an impending layoff or loss of a loved one.

There can be many life events that have an apocalyptic impact. Some are within our control, and others are completely outside of our control. Some are rooted in work; others rooted in family or personal relationships; and some simply are a result of being in the wrong place at the wrong time.

Some may be the result of a natural disaster, or of our own choices and actions.

An "apocalypse," generically speaking, is an event involving disruption, destruction or damage on an awesome or catastrophic scale.

What elevates an event to Personal Apocalypse status is the feeling that one's life and belief system is completely shaken on a catastrophic level. It is the magnitude of the impact on an individual's emotional, cognitive and embodied self-experiential level that determines whether or not it rises to the level of a PA, not the intrinsic magnitude of the event itself.

What constitutes a Personal Apocalypse to one may not be a personal apocalypse to another.

A Personal Apocalypse
is not defined by the event itself, but
rather by the experiential impact of the event on the
individual.

The following list offers some events that could serve as the source for experiencing a PA.

Work Related

- Employment
  - Firing or layoff
  - Employer collapse
- Self-Employed
  - Loss of clients, customers or market demand
  - Expertise or skill set commoditization or obsolescence
  - Lack of required knowledge or know-how

Personal

- Personal crisis
  - Death
  - Divorce
  - Homelessness
  - Bankruptcy
  - Health crisis
  - Spiritual crisis
  - Identity crisis
  - Economic crisis
  - Empty nest

- Accidents
  - Motor vehicle
  - Personal injury
    - Assault
    - Machinery
    - Weapons
    - Athletic

- Social isolation
  - Circumstantial
    - Detention
    - Incarceration
    - Incapacitation
    - Banned from online communities.
    - Banned from social networks.

- Geographic
  - Remote location
  - Deportation
  - Forced migration
  - Immigration
- Technological
  - Blocked from internet access.
  - Lack of connectivity or hardware
- Discriminatory
  - Gender
  - Race
  - Ethnic origin
  - Faith
  - Sexual identity
  - Appearance
  - Challenge
  - Political orientation

- Consequences of choices & actions
  - Failed investments
  - Bad selection of:
    - Partners
    - Friends
    - Clients

Disasters

- Natural
  - Pandemics
  - Flood
  - Fire
  - Earthquake
  - Tsunami
  - Volcano
  - Storms

- Manmade
  - Political collapse
  - Economic collapse
  - Social disintegration
  - Technology failure
  - Civil disorder
  - Military conflict

PA Events Versus Other Significant Life Events

There are many transformational life events that can carry with them a sense of profound loss or significant fear, but do not rise to the level of a PA.

For some, the birth of a first child, or the prospect of getting married can provoke significant anxiety. However, it would be less likely that they would be experienced as traumatic by most people.

A PA will involve significant psychological, physical, or circumstantial loss, often on a large scale. It will also tend to trigger fear, as an immediate and reflexive response.

PA events are often unexpected, in terms of timing. Even if I know that I am at risk of being fired, the actual moment I receive notice is outside of my control.

Events leading up to the PA may be sudden and completely without warning, or they can be internalized over a longer period of time, without triggering an attempt at avoidance.

An example might be like a tsunami appearing on the horizon where people stand and stare, not recognizing the danger until the wave is upon them. The moment of truth is something that defies preparation or avoidance.

As with the timing above, the magnitude of reaction to an apocalyptic event can be completely unpredictable and unforeseen.

This book may not be helpful for someone in the middle of an apocalyptic event. Conversely, it also may not provide value to someone already well on the road to recovery after such an event.

This book is most helpful for those who find themselves still alive and kicking in the wake of experiencing a PA but find it extremely challenging to get traction and movement toward building a new life.

The PA Impact

Each of us has our own unique experiential "operating system." The vulnerability of that operating system to a crash is also unique to each of us. The threshold for when a PA becomes personally and profoundly affecting is just as unique.

The magnitude of the reaction to an apocalyptic event can be immediate or delayed, conscious or unconscious, completely debilitating or not, numbing or nightmarish, episodic or recurrent.

The common thread is that these experiences are not within our control; and, they can often defy any efforts to assert control or resistance over their effects.

Extreme cases are beyond the scope of this book, and we defer to clinical and psychological professionals for those affected. This would be as in the case of those diagnosed with Post Traumatic Stress Disorder (PTSD). In these cases specialized treatment is required.

The reason for qualifying these extreme consequences as falling outside of our scope, is that the people suffering from these conditions may, in the moment, lack the capacity to engage in a process of life reconstruction, until they have gotten past the trauma of the apocalyptic event itself.

For a significantly larger number of people subjected to a PA in their lives, the effects are often completely internalized for the individual, and they are often invisible to others in their life.

Someone who experiences a PA can react either from a place of acceptance or denial. Those around the person can react from a place of acknowledgment and caring, or denial and judgment, with the latter exacerbating the post-PA impacts.

Regardless of the magnitude of the impact experienced, it can be valuable to seek advice and support from others. This can be friends, family, professional service providers, faith-based support providers, peer support communities, books, courses, workshops, and programs.

Using these resources carries no judgment nor stigma. The very real impact of a PA in one's life is no less significant than any other emergent experience.

We do not hesitate to call a doctor, or emergency plumber or electrician, when the need arises. It is second nature. However, in the face of a PA, the instinct is to go to self-judgment or shame, and resist reaching out for help.

The Natural Post-PA Response

The natural response to a PA can be to experience significant stress, fear, and disorientation, often accompanied by an all-consuming sense of powerlessness and isolation.

In today's culture, our value and identity are inextricably tied to our productivity, the achievement of tangible results, and our accomplishments. The experience of the loss of a job or obsolescence of a skill or profession can be just as devastating as the loss of our home in a natural disaster.

Personal losses, whether of a spouse, due to an accident or a personal health crisis, can strike at the core of our beliefs about self-worth, identity, confidence, abilities, and understanding of our place in the world.

This can be made worse by self-judgment(s) or judgments of others- of failure, inadequacy and direct personal responsibility. Not just for what happened and its related consequences, but for our failure to successfully avoid it, or to navigate successfully through it.

Many cultures place a huge premium on "looking good." This can be expressed by our appearance, our possessions, our social status, or our activities. Attempting to keep up with these expectations can amplify the emotional crisis caused by a PA.

Socio-cultural pressures and expectations of those around us, both real and imagined, can serve to increase the pressure to immediately move into action. This, often in service to maintaining the appearance of normality and success.

Each context, whether work, family, friends, followers, clubs, or religious institutions, carries its own unique set of expectations and demands.

Maintaining a façade of credibility and success post-PA is a heavy burden and a tax on time and attention critically needed to meet immediate challenges; and, it is a drain on physical, emotional, mental, and spiritual strength and resilience.

The effect of social pressure diminishes the capacity for self-reflection and the capacity to process the emotional and spiritual effects.

Encouraging action, rather than supporting the grieving and processing time that is necessary, reinforces the influence and impact of the PA.

Another example of these effects on judgment can be distorted perceptions that result in exaggerated or diminished responsiveness to incoming signals and new situations.

Everything from listening and comprehension, to responding and interacting with others can be affected, thus resulting in insensitive, or inappropriate understanding, and causing harmful or destructive actions and unintended consequences.

In the midst of the post-PA experience, whether at full force immediately after, or as a slow boil over time, we are culturally expected to rise from the ashes, rally, and find the clarity, strength and ability to triumph and achieve a miraculous recovery.

Tales of those who have overcome the most horrendous personal traumas and tragedies abound, with heroic successes and achievements. These stories can be the source of both powerful inspiration and motivation.

There is an old adage that says, "if you compare your inside to someone else's outside, you will always lose." Under the PA's influence, the tendency to compare oneself with others can be amplified and exaggerated, deepening self-judgment and self-criticism.

This self-reinforcing self-judgment and self-condemnation anchors the focus on what was pre-PA, and what has been lost. The result is a diversion of energy and resources from responding to the present circumstance. Living with our eyes glued to the rear- view mirror reinforces the grip of the PA.

When we focus on the past, our future is colored by the PA story we construct for ourselves. Lots of opportunities and possibilities are swept off the table by fears and unfounded beliefs, such as, "I am too old to pursue this," "I cannot learn this at my age," or "It is too late for me to start all over."

Ready, Fire, Aim

The first instinct in the wake of a PA is to look for something, *anything* that might provide immediate salvation for the circumstantial challenges we are facing.

Offers and resources abound, with programs, services, advice, trainings, elixirs, diets, paths to riches, paths to spiritual awakening, products, support groups, workshops, any and all of which hold the promise of a cure.

The temptation is to grab onto the nearest first thing at hand, like a life preserver thrown to a drowning man. This is completely understandable, given the desperate circumstances being experienced.

Here is a typical example of how a PA could play out. With full commitment and desire to fix what ails, you pick yourself up, dust yourself off, and zero in on one of the choices, roll up your sleeves, and put your shoulder to the wheel.

After some period of time, with no tangible results, you switch to an alternative fix: you purchase a program, start an Internet business, only to be met with the sound of chirping crickets.

After a meaningful commitment of time, attention and resources, you realize this is another dry well.

You then decide to change course and seek guidance from a leader in the field of personal growth and development, or learn an entirely new skill. After several presentations, workshops, consumption of books, and dutiful engagement with checklists and workbooks, you develop and implement a plan. Two months later you are still lacking a tangible result.

It becomes clear that the plan is not working; and, with no intention of giving up, you turn back to the first attempt with new resolve, and the cycle starts anew.

This example reflects a pattern of "ready," "fire," "aim," rather than taking the time to thoughtfully evaluate and analyze the potential risks associated with the decisions being made.

Decisions based on urgency, which escalate to "fight" or "flight" status, are less likely to be rational and more likely to fail.

Within a frame of post-PA insecurity and loss of self-confidence, anyone is susceptible to self-generated beliefs of diminished competencies and capacities.

The rate of change in the world continues to accelerate, intensifying the feeling of personal inadequacy. This renders many possible choices as obsolete or irrelevant as soon as they are chosen and pursued. If the target is continuously receding from view, how is it possible to hit the bullseye?

Fear and Personal Apocalypse

In the post-PA state of perception, all judgement, discernment, and decision-making can be distorted and compressed by fear. This compression is rooted in a survival level urgency.

From a compromised and impaired state of mind, deep within our reptilian brain (the fight or flight part), the strategies, beliefs, and conclusions that will control all of our next choices and actions are formed.

This is the moment when, on an unconscious level, we decide what is and is not possible, what is and is not available or achievable, and what is and is not accessible. These beliefs become fixed anchors framing our view of the world and life going forward.

Recognize that this post-PA moment is one where a powerful array of fears, beliefs, assumptions, and choices are born.

These internalized beliefs can produce misery, from the emotional wellspring from which they emerge-that being fear and scarcity.

Beliefs and stories created in the furnace of personal crisis will unconsciously define and pre-constrain the universe of possibilities going forward.

However, these beliefs and stories are not rooted in objective reality, truth or circumstance. All these beliefs are experientially colored and subjectively created. If you can change the frame, the lens, and the filters, what you perceive will change accordingly.

In this state, post-PA, judgment is the most powerful filter of all in obscuring and distorting one's ability to see, or even conceive of the unlimited array of choices and possibilities that abound.

Confusion of our identity with our results can be another byproduct of judgment. One might think, "If I achieve success, then I am a success, as a human being. If I don't, then I am a failure as a human being." This narrative is culturally pervasive, going back to childhood and early educational paradigms.

Who we are is not equal to our results, our income, or our achievements. We are human beings first, and secondarily, we choose to invest time and attention in service to achieving or creating those results. A person's identity and value as a human being is not defined by their achievements.

Another response to PA after an extended period of failed attempts to navigate a path to self-sustainability is to lose not just confidence, but actual belief in the skills and abilities we used prior to the apocalyptic event.

Take, for example, the PA of being fired from a job that is phased out due to technological advancements. The fact that the context within which one's knowledge, talent, and skills were employed may have disappeared, does not mean that the "I" who possessed those attributes, has lost them.

Between freshly baked fears and anxieties, new beliefs and narratives rooted in scarcity, loss of identity and confidence are formed.

This can be accompanied by a loss of drive, life energy, or focus, even in connection with the most basic chores of day-to-day life much less the challenge of rebuilding one.

Post-PA Self-Awareness

You may ask: "How do I become aware of whether I am in the grip of post-PA's effects?" There are some fundamental questions one can ask.

These are cold-hard-truth-bottom-line types of questions. The answers reveal the truth of one's current circumstance, and one's effectiveness in coping with it, viewed through a results-oriented lens.

These are not profound inquiries into the nature of time, space, and my place in the Universe. These are the types of questions a well-meaning best friend, partner, or spouse might ask, at an intervention, long after a PA.

On the work front:

- How long have I been out of gainful employment, or not paid appropriately for my time or labor?
- How many programs or trainings have I pursued since the PA, that have successfully earned back their cost?

- How many sweat-equity projects or entrepreneurial ventures have I invested time in, or contributed money to that proved to be dry wells?

On the personal front:

- How many personal growth and development programs, workshops, or self-help books have I consumed since the bottom fell out, that failed to provide an experiential or actual benefit?

- How many personal relationships with family, friends, spouse, or partners have been lost, damaged or are currently at risk?

- How many adverse changes in home, car, financial circumstances, ownership of possessions, community profile, personal identity, or social life have happened?

The answers to these questions when separated from their justifications and excuses, represent the true results of one's efforts- the truth of one's current reality in undistorted full technicolor.

The question is not what we have done, are currently considering, or are thinking about doing in the future.

The question is whether the "I" who is making these choices is stuck in a loop of failed results and defeated expectations. If so, then it is likely that you are suffering from post-PA effects.

If this is true for you, then we have some unpacking that might help you navigate the journey beyond your PA. The hope is to help with self-understanding, regaining control over your life; and ultimately, to help you transcend the effects of the PA.

§

TRUE INTROSPECTION

Everyone is familiar with this quote:

> "The definition of insanity is doing the same thing over and over again, but expecting a different result."

Within the PA mindset, I am not out of my mind for doing my best to turn things around; only to find myself going around in circles. It is actually quite the opposite.

Within the PA distortion field, all of my resources, rationality, and creativity are working at full speed. The problem is that a true heading that would get me to the desired destination has been replaced by a mirage that disappears upon arrival.

The mirage is self-generated, and makes the PA effects self-sustaining. It is embodied in the stories I tell myself, and others: "This time is different than before," and "This time it will work."

This traps me in a non-generative, non-productive story; where the characters' names and faces change, but the plot and outcome remain the same.

The challenge is- how do I stop an illusion, and the distortion of my vision and judgment, if I am the one creating and experiencing it?

If there is certainty about what I am sensing and thinking, questioning those perceptions can seem unthinkable. It is only after the Titanic went down, that the designer realized it was not iceberg-proof and unsinkable.

After the 10th, 20th, 30th resumé submission has failed to generate any response, it may be time to seek an outside opinion on why I am missing the mark. Asking for help or guidance here is the better part of valor.

What might account for the pattern of failure and defeated expectations, after the third attempt at going independent with one's own business, without successfully generating a client or sale? Perhaps, here again, it is time to seek guidance or advice.

Before returning to the battlefield, there needs to be a recognition of the effects of a PA on how you think and behave. This means questioning, across the board, everything you think, feel, believe, and do. This is not just about what to do next and how to do it, but on the "I" who is asking.

On a more profound level, what may reside within one's heart and desires, that has been ignored or dismissed as a choice, may in fact hold the key to transforming PA induced beliefs.

On emotional and spiritual levels, there is an array of unconscious fears, beliefs, and shadows that may pre- date the PA, that can be triggered and exacerbated. The post-PA narrative can then be self-generated out of those past fears.

These effects serve to narrow one's field of view, limiting the choices one can see, and even coloring perceived potential benefits as guaranteed returns.

We can all remember the first time we were given a new box of crayons. If it was the jumbo version, there were almost too many colors to choose from. Under post- PA effects, one can only see black and white.

Clearing the boards of any and all non-productive activities may serve to create the time and space for true introspection. The focus is on your self, intentions, goals, desires, and the analysis and evaluation of possible options that actually afford a clear path to a new and improved future.

The "Who" Comes First

Shifting out of post-PA behavioral patterns involves changing how I have been thinking about myself, and my situation. This means a change in focus from *"What to do?"* to *"Who am I?"* and *"What do I want?"*

Clearly answering the first question, "Who am I?" is a prerequisite to getting to the second question of "What do I want?" PA induced behaviors skip both of these questions, shifting the focus to doing something, anything that might provide salvation.

The key is to realize that I am the source of my experience of my life, good, bad or ugly. Recognizing and reconnecting with my power of authorship, ownership and agency is critical to getting out from under the effects of a PA.

Getting to Know Oneself

Reconnecting with your inner power and generative potential, in service to restoring your life's momentum, requires giving yourself the opportunity to look within.

This is easier said than done when the voices in your head are hammering home PA induced fears and beliefs, with whichever one screaming loudest and last winning the attention and priority.

It is also possible for some that this level of introspection may be unprecedented in their lives.

Many of us find our life's path before the occurrence of a PA to have been a naturally unplanned and uncalculated sequence of events: school, higher education, first job, marriage, career; without much time for significant introspection.

On the other hand, there are many whose path seems pre-determined by the legacy of past generations, programmed from early childhood. If one is the fourth generation of firefighter or professional, often relatively little introspection was required to find oneself following the family tradition, whether in a uniform or exam room.

Another facet of getting to know yourself, on a fully embodied and conscious basis, is to recognize the source from which your beliefs, intentions and choices are made.

Your current context can be cast from the heat and pressure of a PA, the loss of an opportunity, or the evaporation of a pre-destiny.

The source is always self-generated and self-sustained. To identify a PA as source, is to awaken your full self- awareness. This awakening defines whether or not you will play those beliefs, intentions and choices forward, or chart a new path.

§

GETTING OUT FROM UNDER

Here is the narrative at the heart of post-PA life: I have experienced a PA and immediately shifted into action; I have set a course to remediate the losses with a strategy, only to find failed expectations and unsatisfactory results with each successive attempt.

The challenge lies in stepping outside of the current experiential frame. Getting out from under the PA, on a core psychological, emotional, and spiritual level requires a fundamentally different frame of reference, and a shift in core beliefs.

Achieving that shift calls for an entirely counterintuitive action.

The following chapters seek to explore elements of an approach to shifting one's orientation, perspective, and beliefs.

Stop Digging

The old adage:

> *"If you find yourself at the bottom of a deep dark hole, the first step towards getting out is to stop digging."*

The same concept applies to post-PA choices and patterns of behavior. Our suggestion is, stop doing what you are doing, take a deep breath, and give yourself the opportunity to re-examine and reevaluate the situation.

This is not about taking a break, taking up meditation, scheduling a few hours of unstructured time, or a weekend of reflection. Stop means stop.

Whatever the current discussions, pressures, or commitments currently keeping you busy, and driving your actions; if you have not already generated success, a tangible result, or progress, you should stop all of them completely.

You might ask yourself: "could this heighten all of the feelings, fears, and reactivities I have, as well as those near and dear to me, who have watched the PA aftermath?" Absolutely. However, the first step to getting out from under is to resist the natural influences of a PA on your life.

It is highly likely that those around you, who are associated with whatever you are now currently engaged with, will have been chosen and positioned by you to keep the post-PA strategy going.

Remember, you cast them in your play, to feed and serve your post-PA fears, beliefs and narratives. This may not have been conscious on your part.

Have no doubt that the post-PA casting of people and projects in your life are in service to a hidden goal: to affirm the stories, fears, beliefs, and perceived limitations born in the wake of the PA.

This post-PA "casting" does not necessarily involve a change or replacement of the people in your life. It can include many of the same people, contexts, relationships, and engagements that pre-existed the PA.

With the after-effects of the PA, the decision to continue with those relationships and engagements can be biased in service to feeding the post-PA

31

narrative, rather than your best interests going forward.

It is not unusual for previous relationships and circumstances to exhibit significant adverse changes as a result of PA influence.

There are two stories post-PA. The story you tell others is, "I am going out to [fill in the blank] in service to recovery and getting back on my feet." However, the inner post-PA narrative: "I have lost everything," "I am incapable of fixing this," or "I am too old and too tired to start again" can be persistent, thus compromising all future attempts at recovery.

The first challenge is to stop doing what has been generating failed results.

The subjective and often delusional truth of people facing post-PA circumstances, is that somehow, their basic needs *are* being met, despite the lack of any tangible results being generated.

The companion thought to the above is that if they take time away from what they are currently doing, their current circumstance will be adversely affected, despite the actual ineffectiveness of current efforts.

Stopping allows you to remove the PA colored glasses, clear your vision, and free your mind to reevaluate your situation.

The empirical truth is- if somehow, you have managed to survive under the influence of a PA, without compromising your living conditions, then you will continue to survive without circumstantial change, in the absence of non-productive commitments and behaviors.

The imperative attached to "being busy," independent of any tangible benefit or result, is at the heart of being trapped within a post-PA frame of reference.

Stopping this merry-go-round and reevaluating and reviewing one's current choices and actions can be experienced as "doing nothing."

This distortion is rooted in an irrational post-PA fear and disorientation. To get back on track, you will need to discern what is rational and effective, and what is tangibly ineffective and delusional.

Letting go of concern for how one looks, in terms of the need to appear busy to others, is critical to realizing the need to create the time and space to do productive internal work.
Stopping means ending the status quo, and shifting into true processing and reflection of: place, circumstance, feelings, beliefs, and perceptions of the human being experiencing all of the above in the present.

There are No Magic Pills

It is common, post-PA, to seek salvation in the form of a pre-packaged offering. These are designed and marketed to appeal to those struggling with post-PA challenges; and appear to provide a one-stop-comprehensive solution.

The risk of sourcing one's salvation externally, is that it can alleviate the symptoms, as long as you continue to buy, attend, or practice; however often without addressing the underlying cause.

It also can result in the "tail wagging the dog," introducing agendas and motivations that are in service to the interests of the providers.

This is not to suggest that these external programs and offerings are intrinsically wrong or of no value. Rather, it is to emphasize the importance of the buyer's understanding, intention, and discernment in resorting to them.

If one is seeking a magic pill, then you are ultimately allowing the PA influence to push you toward these external solutions; and this can divert you from the internal work needed to navigate your way out.

If, on the other hand, these offerings are used to achieve greater self-awareness and understanding of your own PA-provoked behaviors, cognitive biases, fears, and hidden goals; they can provide significant value and tools with which to work.

The mechanism for transcending the post-PA malaise really needs to be of your own design and construction, based on your own preferences, values, and desires. To have your cake and eat it too, it is important that you are the one baking it.

Under the post-PA effects, it is easy to be drawn to and influenced by these external providers, and end up treating symptoms without treating the underlying condition. This can inadvertently add a new dependency to the pile.

Side effects of treating the symptoms instead of the cause can be increased despair, fatigue, and frustration. This then increases the risk of a deepening dependence on third party offerings, as a "doubling down," while eroding one's own self-determination.

At the heart of this lies the risk of losing discernment and discrimination. Questions like, "What am I looking to get from this?"; and "Why am I finding this of interest?" can go unasked and unanswered.

Anesthetic Relief

Clarity of mind, in asking these questions can be sorely lacking from within a PA mediated reality. Habits or dependencies that adversely affect clarity of mind can prevail.

In today's culture, relief through medication or chemical consumption, whether via prescription drugs, recreational drugs, alcohol, illegal substances, stimulants, or endorphin-generating addictive behaviors, can all serve to cloud or muddy self-awareness and feelings, compromising mental clarity.

Seeking relief via these means can serve to perpetuate the PA derived effects, by dampening your senses, and dulling your wits.

Clearly, prescribed pharmaceutical support is not discretionary, and should not be changed or interrupted.

While consuming non-prescribed substances, or engaging in addictive behaviors, there is often no internal capacity to address one's post-PA state of mind and being.

You are not Alone

Creating the time, space, and resources to take a personal inventory, and shift into conscious awareness of what you have been doing, diverting, or ducking is why this "stop digging" piece is so critical.

Confrontation with self, truth and reality can be an extremely bitter pill to swallow. The goal is not to engage in self-blame or self-judgment about who you are, post-PA.

The goal is to gain clarity on what to think and do next, in service to transcending the PA; and what information, insight and understanding can be used to move forward.

It is important to remember that you have brought yourself to this point; and have lived to tell the tale.

Now you have the opportunity to change the program going forward.

Part of the PA generated beliefs is that I am alone in the struggle; and, it is my problem to solve, without any help or support from others. This can be a side effect of the aforementioned "looking good"-while-Rome- burns behavior touched on previously.

This belief can profoundly impact your awareness, perception, and ability to process signals from people around me who could help.

Some may actively offer to help. Others, who would respond if asked or invited, may feel hesitant about stepping up because of the self-reliant energy you are projecting.

In response to an offer of help, a typical response might be, "I appreciate your offer, but I am fine, and everything is okay." For those who might be waiting for a sign or signal from you, after your response, they may become distant, less responsive or available, sending the message of being too busy or disinterested.

Often, you can communicate and act in ways that amplify the feeling of isolation, unintentionally missing offers of help or assistance.

Being stuck in the post-PA state can be a dynamic equilibrium. You are constantly in motion and action trying to improve your situation; and simultaneously being affected by all the compounding effects on identity, self-confidence, and lived reality. This is akin to taking one step forward, and then two steps back.

The moral of this is that there are many limiting beliefs operating, often unconsciously, to sustain and preserve a PA derived narrative when it is running the show.

Recognizing these limitations enables you to decide what to stop doing, and how to change.

> *"It is impossible to clean your eyeglasses while holding them by the lens."*

Doug Breitbart

Creating a Blank Slate

After reading this far, you may realize that you have experienced an event in your life that rose to the level of a PA, and you may or may not have taken the first step toward expanded self-awareness.

The goal is to uncover and hopefully stop reflexive choices and actions from defining your future, and to create the space, time and attention to inventory and adjust your current circumstances.

Clearing the boards and creating a blank slate, to look at one's life is no easy task; however, before you can renovate your current life, the old fixtures must be removed, the frame exposed, and an inventory of what is in need of repair or replacement, done.

Resetting the stage, and enabling the formulation of the what, where, how, when and with whom you want to create the next chapter of your life is fundamental to getting past the PA.
The goal is to do so in as self-realized, embodied, and conscious a way as possible going forward.

§

YOU AS SOURCE

Let's look at the question, "Where do I begin?" There are two ways of reading this question. There is the "where" do I begin, as in "what to do first, where do I start?" Or is the focus on the "I," in terms of self- awareness and boundaries, as in "where do I begin and end in relation to myself, others, and the world around me?"

This is fundamentally subjective. Only the self can answer this, as the ultimate authority over one's life and choices. It chooses and ultimately manifests everything on a person's life stage: the good, the bad and the ugly.

This does not mean that all PAs are within anyone's control to avoid or prevent. As the old saying goes, "Sh*t happens." John Lennon had a famous quote: "Life is what happens to you while you're planning."

Clearly no one asks to be the victim of a PA; however, the moment of choice immediately post-PA, in terms
of how we choose to respond and react is 100% within our discretion and control.

The when, where, how, why and with whom those choices are made may, or may not be the product of conscious choice, nor with full awareness of underlying intentions or motivations.

However, there is no higher authority than you, when it comes to your life, how you live it, the decisions you make, the actions you take, and the consequences that are generated.

Fear or Love

What is the source underlying my choices, whether consciously or unconsciously made? We believe, for the purpose of transcending PA effects, that there are only two primal emotional sources out of which choices are made-- love or fear.

When we look back at the choices made and consequences generated over the course of our lives, and dig deeply enough to identify the core underlying source of each of those choices; ultimately either fear or love will have been tapped.

When fear is the root of a choice, it will generally result in consequences that reinforce that fear. This is the basis upon which PA induced fears and beliefs are self- sustaining.

On the other hand, when love is the source, the choices and consequences map to abundance and positive affirmation. There is a sense of safety, and openness to possibility.

To transcend fear-based thinking, one cannot use a strategy that is based on fear. The first challenge is to shed the fears and limiting beliefs.

Fears and negative beliefs derive their power and effect by manifesting in the form of limiting thoughts, like "I'm too old", "I'm too unskilled", "It is too late", "I'm not strong enough", or "I'm not good enough."

These fear-rooted thoughts define a person's words and actions, and can dictate the reality that affirms them.

It is impossible to manifest something you believe is unachievable. As Henry Ford said,

*"Whether you think you can,
or you think you can't,
you're right."*

How Does it Work?

Our generative potential in any given moment, is directly related to how we frame our thoughts, words and actions. How does this work? How do beliefs, thoughts, words and actions interrelate, in the context of defining, expressing and creating a post-PA life?

The first step to creating the life we want is to have a vision of that life.

It is common for people to confront the reality of their lives, not as a product of their own doing, but as an external circumstance beyond their control. Emotions generate beliefs, beliefs inform thoughts, those thoughts lead to words, words lead to actions, and actions produce results. This creative process can be vicious or virtuous, depending upon the emotional source.

Connecting the dots, from source belief to end result can be extremely challenging. The belief generates a result that affirms itself, then queues up the next iteration, and operates as a self-reinforcing generative pattern.

These cycles can operate completely unconsciously, independent of whether the outcome is virtuous or catastrophic.

On Beliefs

The word "belief," in its original use, found its root in the idea of holding something dear, in high esteem, or trust. Other root meanings invoked care, desire, and love.

By the mid-16th century, belief had become limited in meaning to "mental acceptance of something as true."

In our current context, a belief is an individually held and fully embodied truth that defines how one filters their perception of reality.

A belief is a subjectively created and held perceptual understanding, or "knowing," that is the result of our need, in the face of a traumatic event, to rationalize the cause of both the event itself, and the emotional response to it.

In creating the narrative, the belief provides a feeling of control and self-protection. When next confronted with similar events and triggered fears, one now knows the what, why and how to cope with that experience.

If the belief is foundational and about oneself; then it can be applied broadly to many events in the future that trigger it.

The narrative underlying any particular belief may or may not be objectively true; however, its effectiveness is unaffected by whether it is based in fact or not.

Change the Belief, Change the Result

If you want to change the result, then you probably should start by focusing on the beginning of the process, and the fears and beliefs that produced it.

Clearing self-imposed limitations and scarcity-based fears enables you to generate new affirming beliefs about yourself, your life, relationships, skills, talents, superpowers, and potential going forward.

Taking the temperature of your current state of being, happens through your own self-awareness and a commitment to do this inventory without judgments, filters, fantasies, wishful thinking, or self-delusions.

There are a myriad number of exercises, tools and resources available to assist you with this process; and how you might approach the rebuilding that follows this kind of spiritual and emotional house cleaning.

However, without a full commitment to get to the bottom of your fears, beliefs, and truth; it is easy to inadvertently reinforce the rationale for remaining under the influence of post-PA fears and beliefs.

The key to getting out from under the effects of the PA is the commitment to actually do oneself differently.

Our innate superpower is our ability to take charge of and change our beliefs, eliminate fear from the equation, and write a new story for our lives.

Finding the Unconscious Culprits

If fear-based beliefs are affecting your thoughts; then rooting out those fears and limiting beliefs is required to change the result.

A question that often arises is "Why would I continue to "ask" for failed results?" Clearly no one would seek a series of failed outcomes, no matter how well intentioned the effort is in generating them. To get a handle on why serial failures keep happening, it can be helpful to shift one's perspective from a subjective lens to an as-objective-as-possible rational view of what has been going on.

If you take the judgments and blaming out of the equation, and focus on the source and sequence of the creative process at work, it can make it easier to identify the hidden drivers.

These drivers can often be rooted in beliefs formed long before the PA. It may well be that the PA served to trigger their re-activation.

An analogy would be to view our psyche as if functioning like a computer, with our operating system being written and augmented as we process our life experiences- the new incoming data.

Most of the operating system is built up and coded without challenge in relation to the incoming data.

However, the 10% to 15% of those experiences that trigger a traumatic emotional response are the basis for new fear-based code being inserted into the operating system as a belief.

This belief is then triggered when presented with similar contexts and experiences.

These triggers are like programs, usually embedded deep within our operating system when we are very young; and over time, they run in the background.

Additional layers of new operating system code, and new applications are built up on the layers below as we age, pushing the source code of embedded fears and beliefs deeper into the subconscious.

How does this relate to stopping PA triggered consequences?

If these sections of the operating system are being run subconsciously, how does one locate them, in service to replacing them with new code?

Clearly, we do not have a reset button, that enables us to reconfigure our reactions and choices.

What we do have is a series of results that we experienced as undesirable and unanticipated; with absolutely no idea where, how or why things went wrong.

By starting from these outcomes and working backwards, it is possible to identify the source belief that produced them.

Remember that we get exactly what we ask for, literally. If you accept that all results you experience are the product of your own engineering; then, a failed result can serve to affirm a subconsciously embedded fear or negative belief.

We are not used to looking at bad things through an affirmative lens; however, it can be valuable to recognize that a negative belief caused the negative result, to affirm itself.

So, as an example, if your belief is that you are uniquely unworthy and unentitled to be acknowledged as a valuable contributor; then you would avoid contexts and opportunities where that would happen.

Or you might attribute credit to others, in service to deflecting acceptance of recognition or acknowledgment.

When this is operating on a subconscious level, the outcome is never to receive credit for a job well done. Your thought and expression are, "See, I never get credit for my work."

Connecting that outcome to the choices and actions taken to assure it is never obvious. Without understanding how one's actions connect beliefs to results, it is guaranteed that the results will never change

independent of one's best efforts to do so. This affirmation of a subconscious belief is what we refer to as a hidden goal.

Leaving the "how" that negative result occurred as a result of thoughts, words, and actions unexamined, is what serves to preserve the subconscious source belief.

By making the source belief explicit, it affords the opportunity to decide whether or not to change it. Reflected in that result is one's truth. That truth, as an embodied belief, is the negative operating system being run.

Examine the failed result, calculate backwards to the source belief being affirmed, and the negative code can be identified and replaced. This examination can benefit by seeking support and insights from others.

Change the source belief, realign the thoughts, words and actions derived from it, and the result is guaranteed to change.

Seeing the events and emergent consequences through this authorship lens can involve reconnecting with one's own personal power: You might say,

"I have the ability to choose what I believe, think, say and do; and to take responsibility for the results I generate."

Remember the earlier reference to the source of our beliefs? They are rooted in either fear and scarcity, or love and abundance.

Even when rooted in fear, once a belief is embedded and operating, every thought, word and action taken thereafter will have, as its first and greatest driver, the affirmation of its own validity.

Our negative beliefs originate circumstantially out of what we perceive to be life and death moments. Fear arises in the face of perceived threats to our survival.

The belief that is formed carries that level of core life-or-death conviction.

Replacing a fear-based belief with a love-based self-affirming one, on an experiential level, is more akin to a heart transplant than removal of one's tonsils.

The part being replaced has served as a core belief central to your survival up to that point. Its change will be experienced, on a psychological and emotional level, as a life-threatening event.

Identifying and recognizing a negative belief you have about yourself or in relation to the world, that has been affirmed over and over again by achieving the same adverse result, goes to the heart and soul of post-PA patterns.

We know a negative belief maps directly to a negative outcome or result. We also know that a string of negative results bearing resemblances and similarities between them both in context and consequence makes a pattern.

Within that pattern lay the same core thoughts, words and actions that produced it. The question that begs to be asked is, by achieving that string of negative results, what truth or belief about yourself have you affirmed?

By taking the rationalization as to why this particular failure was unique and different out of the equation; it is easier to recognize the resemblance of this event to a series of previous results, all affirming the same core belief.

This series of results is a reflection of your creative capacity to prove yourself right. This, despite the reality that what you are affirming is a negative belief about yourself.

Those beliefs, if subconscious, actually operate as the generator of hidden goals; turned on when confronted with an opportunity to flex their muscles.

There are lots of tools, resources, and offerings available to assist us with the introspective and investigative process of inventorying our results, choices, words and actions, and interpreting those results with fresh eyes.

All of this is ultimately in service to identifying those portions of your operating system that no longer serve to create the life you want.

The Importance of Being Explicit

Once you have confronted and cleared your limiting beliefs, the process of getting used to abundant and self-affirming new beliefs requires one more step-defining the kind of life you want to create.

Some have gone through this process before; however; for many, it may in fact be the first time on a conscious and deliberate basis that they actually sit down and put pen to paper, endeavoring to describe the life they want.

The first step in the creative process is to have a vision for the life to be. The second step is to express that vision as an explicit request articulated and "published" beyond the confines of one's head. It is guaranteed that if you do not ask for what you want, you will not get it.

In order for the request to register, the expression has to be converted into a tangible or perceptual form that others are capable of perceiving or sensing. If the vision stays silently locked within one's mind, there will be no mechanism for it to manifest in the world.

Progressing from a vision to an expression is the intermediate step to bringing that vision to life. This "publication" piece, the articulation of what you want to create, usually manifests through language, although artistic expression can be equally powerful, regardless of media or form of artifact.

Whether written, recorded, or drawn, there are many offerings available to help you with the creative process of imagining and expressing the future you would like to create.

This process is not a test. Asking for support or help from others in surfacing and focusing your request can also be invaluable; however, it is important that the helper does not color or distort your "ask" with their own agenda and desires.

The language or imagery used in the expression will be a literal reflection of what you want. Expressions in that description can be either disempowering or empowering.

Statements rooted in assertive, positive and results-oriented language are more likely to lead to achievement of that goal or vision.

If your goal is to find employment, and your statement is, "I want a job," the literal translation of that statement is that you are asking for a whole lot of "wanting." If you statement is, "I will find a job within the next five days"; then it is empowered, specific, and likely to result in you having that job within that time frame.

Recognizing the power of language, and self-awareness of word choices, is central to identifying whether one is being affected by post-PA thinking, or free of it.

Defining your core values, preferences, passions, and abilities is not a process for the faint of heart. It requires raising to full consciousness the responsibility you bear.

Not just to define the life you want, but also to own and be accountable for the results and consequences you generate, based on the language you used to ask for it.

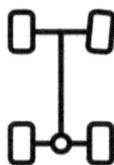

On Alignment

Once you have defined and expressed a post-PA vision for your life, the last step is to take the necessary actions to make that vision a reality. The goal is for those actions to be aligned. This alignment is central to getting exactly what you ask for.

What happens when the wheels on a car are misaligned? As you drive, the steering requires constant adjustment and correction to stay in lane. If you get distracted, the ditch at the side of the road awaits. Misalignment of thoughts, words and actions is no different.

If my thoughts, words and actions are identical, there is very little possibility for the result I ask for not to happen. This concept of concurrence of my thoughts and my words, my words and my actions means that they are aligned.

Any deviation between them, thought to word, or word to action (usually the result of fear-based doubts or beliefs) will virtually guarantee a result that falls short of the stated goal or misses the mark completely.

Under post-PA effects, most of the defeated expectations and successive experiences of failed past efforts can be traced back to unconscious misalignment of thoughts, words and actions. Most likely, the original thought was generated out of fear-based limiting beliefs.

So how do you know whether you are engaged in an aligned, non-fear-rooted, non-PA-affected course of action going forward?

Firstly, you can look at the time and attention invested in formulating the new vision. If it leans toward impulsive and reflexive, then buyer beware.

Secondly, in the expression of that vision, does the language reflect scarcity or abundance as a statement of intention? Lastly, are you in action, doing all that you can do in service to bringing your vision to life?

If everything is in alignment, then the results envisioned should be the results realized.

If you find yourself in resistance or doubt, procrastinating, or without tangible results to show, your awareness of the creative process described above
can be used to self-diagnose the source of misalignment that is taking you off course.

This exercise can be challenging, in terms of figuring out how to apply it in one's life. There are many offerings and resources available, complete with workbooks, questionnaires, and templates to assist with this process.

Our suggestion would be to find which ones are right for you, through trial and error, in service to supporting you in this inquiry.

Who I Am Versus What I Do

The next piece of this puzzle is to figure out where you want to go, and who you want to be when you get there.

Within one's life, there is a place, a life purpose, social and professional relationships, resources, and constraints; all interrelated and interdependent.

These are the results of the choices made about what you want. The underlying drivers are rooted in where one experiences passion and connection.

Defining yourself by what you love and who you want to be in the world, rather than by what you do, involves a shift in consciousness. Focusing on love and intention is key to transcendence of PA effects, and honors the heart and passion that defines who you are.

Equating your identity with what you do can subordinate or ignore the human being you are. If you equaled your results, then a failed result would mean you are a failure as a human being.

Escaping the post-PA frame and effects requires recognition that you are not your results; but rather that you are the one who is in control of the fear that can affect them.

In service to not repeating the sins of the past, the journey to be mapped can reflect a 100% aligned result, born out of love, abundance, and coherence with one's core values and greatest passion.

Once out from under the PA's effects, you have the opportunity to not just "recover," but to thrive and realize your true generative potential.

For many the concept of true abundance, on a fully internalized basis can be a completely alien experience. The messaging of our culture, particularly in the West, is rooted in suppression of individual entitlement, and judgment of those who speak up or make demands.

Add to this fundamental competitive imprinting that drives fear and suspicion of others. We are taught early on that obedience to authority is required, independent of any internal values or judgments to the contrary.

Breaking free of a PA's effects requires shedding this early childhood programming that says, "I am not entitled to ask for what I want." Mapping the journey, this time around, affords you the opportunity to explore true abundance, starting with asking the Universe for what you want.

In painting a vision for the life-to-be, free of limiting beliefs; recognize that you have unlimited choices. Think of it as if you gave yourself a blank check to explore, experience and excel in every aspect of your life.

You are the creator of your life; and, there is no higher authority, nor third-party judge, jury or executioner other than you, to define what is right for you.

There is no prescription nor right or wrong, in relation to: where you choose to start, what you choose to prioritize, who you choose to include; and when and where things must occur.

This also is not a one-time-only event. It is a dynamic process, subject to change or modification at will in real time as you go.

Bringing urgency into the equation, not from a place of fear, but rather joy, excitement and anticipation can also serve as a powerful driver.

The old adage "If not now, when, if not you, who?" applies. If the end of this quest is to create the life you want, and leave behind the stagnation of living under post-PA impacts, then there is no reason to wait.

§

Conscious Choice and The New You

We have previously asked "Where do I begin?" and the two ways it can be interpreted. People's tendency is to focus on "what" to do first, rather than the "who," who is doing it.

Self-inquiry, as it relates to visions and entitlement requires looking at how you make decisions.

You might ask,

- "What are my values in relation to others and the world around me?"

- "What are my comfort zones, boundaries, and preferences when connecting and interacting with others?"

- "What do I like and care about the most on an embodied level?"

- "What do I find the most challenging or triggering, in my day-to-day interactions and life experiences?"

- "What are the items that have been on my lifelong to-do list, in service to transforming my health, appearance, attitudes, feelings, habits, relationships, and beyond?"

The reason for asking these or similar questions is because, at least up until now, your aspirations may or may not have been out of alignment with your actions or results.

Now that you are focusing on you in the present, creating the life you want; you can take the opportunity to bring into alignment your new thoughts, words and actions going forward.

In the first moment after transcending the PA's initial effects, it is not as if you are magically freed of all of their drivers.

However, in that moment, you get to review, redefine, and re-contextualize all of the negative or missing elements in your life, freed of the judgments and cognitive biases that contributed to their creation.

Indecision and the Moment of Truth

It is in this moment of choice that you have a moment of truth- do you wipe the slate clean and start from scratch, or do you fall back to the familiar patterns that held you hostage post-PA?

It is not unusual for people, in this moment, to find themselves frozen in indecision. The choice: fear of jumping into a completely undefined future, versus remaining in a familiar but no longer tolerable past.

It is important to recognize the difference between being stuck in a post-PA belief system, versus being stuck in indecision. The former is substantially unconscious, with many of one's choices and actions occurring reflexively.

The latter is the product of a true personal transitional moment, happening within a heightened state of self- awareness and consciousness, even if a challenging one.

People's tendency is to mistake the feelings and experiences of indecision as a continuation of the PA's effects, which can then be used as a rationalization for falling back into familiar patterns and habits.

Recognizing the feelings of indecision as a temporary experience is key to successfully pushing through the fear of the new. Some feelings of being stuck in indecision can be: fatigue, lack of motivation, frustration, and hopelessness. It can be an extremely low energy existential state.

Most of these effects are the result of the indecision itself. One is not fully influenced or controlled by the post-PA beliefs; nor is one actively engaged with writing a new story. It is effectively being frozen between these two states in paralysis.

Pushing through the fear of the unknown, and getting into purposeful new action can immediately lift the lethargy indecision produces.

The shifting of experiential gears is from action taken under the influence of PA-induced beliefs, with all of the attendant distortion and misdirection, to action taken with an open mind, revealing and experiencing a clear emergent future.

A true experiential shift to a new belief system means diving into and taking action in a completely new reality. There are no projections of future scenarios, familiar landmarks, indicators of success, previously held paradigms, nor fantasies or delusions.

Without post-PA induced fears and beliefs serving as the hidden agenda to be affirmed; the new path forward can be rooted in learning, discovery, curiosity, and engagement.

Just a reminder, help with navigating this brave new world is all around you.

To gather all of the pieces that comprise this moment of choice. In summary:

- There is the driver of "being sick and tired of being sick and tired" in relation to the old paradigms and patterns constructed in the wake of the PA.

- There is the fear of stepping into a completely unknown new territory, devoid of any points of familiarity or reference.

- There are the subjective, illusory, and experientially debilitating effects of being frozen, like a deer in the headlights, in indecision about whether to go back or move forward.

At this point, you might legitimately ask, "I thought you were going to help me here. Seems like what you are telling me is that the hole I'm in is deeper and darker than even I thought it was."

The answer for navigating your way through these shadows lies with your own innate ability to make new choices. The first choice on the list becomes, "It's time for me to create a new future."

It is also recognition that the feeling, "I cannot stop doing what I'm doing. If I stop moving, I'm over and done" is based on fear, not objective reality.

It is ultimately your choice whether to play the past forward, or write a new story. There is no right or wrong, good or bad judgement, nor higher authority in relation to the choice you make, other than your own.

The important question for you is whether each decision is a result of conscious self-reflection, and due consideration before you make it; or, a reflexive decision driven by fearful beliefs and judgments rooted in a post-PA operating system.

The choice, and vast array of micro-decisions and actions involved, in generating a new result is secondary to the *you* who is making those decisions.

There are an infinite number of dimensions one can explore. Any initial questions that energize you in the introspective process are valuable. The following are offered as examples:

- Who am I?

- What do I want for my life?

- What are my needs?

- What do I have to offer?

- How do I want to provide it to the world?

Finding the answers to these questions is an inside-out process. Ultimately, you have to seek answers from your truth, your heart, your tastes and preferences, independent of any outside influence.

Who am I?

There are two approaches for this introspective journey. The first is emergent and generative; based on engaging one's imagination from a sensing and feeling place.

Starting with a blank sheet of paper, define all of the dimensions of who you want to be; for instance: what excites and motivates you? What do you have to offer to the world and to those around you?

The picture which emerges may or may not bear any resemblance to the life you have led up till now. That is because a creative self-inquiry represents a blank check opportunity. Often past plans can be limited by many cognitive biases and beliefs that are no longer relevant.

The second approach is to stick your toe in the water. It is more investigatory and rooted in the mindset of taking a life inventory.

The challenge while taking stock of your life, is to leave the rose-colored glasses at home. Clear eyed and authentic self-recognition and acknowledgment of skills, talents, preferences, and personality is the goal.

This latter approach involves looking at what you have, where you are, where you want to be, and what may be missing or dissatisfying for what you want your life to look like.

If you pursue this approach, the idea is not to affirm previous visions and plans; but rather, to check-in with yourself on a clean slate basis.
This, in service to surfacing your truth here and now. The idea is to make sure that what you are about to ask for is actually what you want.

Knowing the new you, post-PA, necessarily includes the good, the bad, and the ugly. It is only with true clarity and honest self-evaluation that a grounded life- transforming journey is enabled. This, without risk or fear of being derailed or disappointed.

This is not to say that adverse things outside of your control may not happen in the future. The aspiration is to eliminate self-inflicted negative consequences that are within your ability to avoid.

What are My Values?

Why start with values? Our personally held values are an expression and reflection of our core beliefs; and, ultimately our values underlie our thoughts, words, and actions, infusing the life we generate.

Here we would like to distinguish personally held values from "value" as a reflection of worth -in monetary or other forms. We would also like to distinguish personal values from cultural add-ins or impositions like religious faith, spiritual practice, laws, codes of conduct or morality, philosophical belief systems, norms, or dogmas.

The values we have in mind are those that serve as the channel through which one's thoughts, words, and actions flow.

This is distinct from context-specific "values" that serve as the basis for projecting judgments of good or bad, right or wrong, approval or disapproval of others.

Here, we are focusing on those of one's values that inform how one perceives, and how one is perceived by others in the world.

Examples might be: do no harm, do unto others what you would want them to do unto you, be true to your word, give without expectations, and receive with gratitude.

What are My Superpowers?

You have unique aptitudes, capabilities, and generative potential to positively contribute to the world. Your innate gifts may or may not have been realized in your life up till now.

This can be from lack of opportunity to discover one's superpowers; or, it can result from one's fear-based beliefs driving the choices being made.

These choices may have been based upon what we thought we should have done, or on judgments affected by perceived risks or dangers associated with following our heart.

This question allows you to distinguish between what you have been doing versus what you actually want to do. The idea is to distinguish between your greatest gifts and talents, versus what you acquired as a skill, but holds no particular appeal.

The interesting telltale, when looking for your superpower, is that it often is the ability you have that you do not consider significant or special, because it comes to you easily without apparent effort.

This tendency to devalue your superpowers can be based on an assumption that what comes easily to you is equally easy for everyone else, so clearly that ability is not particularly remarkable.

The fact that it comes naturally to you is what makes it a superpower. In looking into what your superpower may be, it can be extremely helpful to ask the people in your life what it is they value most about you, or your abilities.

What do I Want?

In the context of asking for what you want, you will get, exactly what you ask for. If you ask for tea, you will get tea.

If the basis for your request is rooted in what you believe is or is not possible, or what is expected or required by others; it does not change the result- you will get what you ask for whether or not it is what you truly want.

There is a universe of fear-based beliefs and self-limiting assumptions that can explain why you might ask for something that is not in fact what you want.

The purpose of asking, "What do I like?" is to replace all the self-generated rules, judgments and assumptions for not getting what you want, with what you actually want.

This is truly a blank-check opportunity. There is no cost or risk in expressing, on paper or out loud, what you want and what you like, on an unconditional basis.

Reconnecting with your right to ask for what you truly want; and, recognizing your ability to ask for it, is the first step to making it manifest. The generative process of expressing and manifesting anything starts with the thought or vision you have.

The basic process is: first think it; second, express it; and third, take the actions to bring it into being.

We are culturally programmed either to not ask, or to root the request in fear and scarcity. Eliminating the fear and scarcity, and the limitations they bring from the equation, can result in an exponential increase in the choices available.

Beware of One's Own Fake News

Self-generated beliefs and judgments about what you can and cannot do post-PA are generally not based on objective reality.

That is not to say that the context that gave birth to them was not real; however, the beliefs one can construct as a result of that context can be materially distorted and often false.

You can choose to give yourself the opportunity to put all your limiting beliefs aside. Through self-inquiry, asking others about their perceptions of you, and exploration of previously dismissed pursuits, you can frame a more authentic you, and reveal what may be possible.

If you previously believed you could not do something and attempted it anyway, it is likely you did that as a way to confirm your perceived lack of ability, and that you should not have tried to do it in the first place. The hidden goal was to affirm the negative belief.

However, without those limiting beliefs, it is possible for you to revisit the idea of doing things previously attempted, in service to finding out what you actually can do, and what is possible now.

In the same vein, if there were things undertaken in the past that have always seemed challenging to do, you can take a look at how you have been doing what you have been doing; and whether there might be other ways of doing the same things, working smarter not harder.

The shift in both of the above contexts is to recognize how the post-PA-constructed hidden goals and beliefs have affected your results, triggering and confirming negative self-perceptions.

With the investment of a little time and attention applied to how you have been doing what you have been doing, you can surface new opportunities.

Another rich source of self-generated fake news and negative belief confirmation, can be others around you with whom you have chosen to populate your life.

A useful analogy might be to view your life as a large-scale Broadway musical; where you are the book writer, composer, producer, director, casting agent, conductor, and investor.

Everything, and everybody who appears on the stage of your life, from when you open your eyes in the morning to when you close them at night, is placed there by your hand in service to performing the story you have chosen to tell.

The people you choose and find yourself in the company of: friends, intimate partners, acquaintances, employers, colleagues, business partners, and family members, amongst others are all like mirrors. They are there in service to reflecting back and confirming your internal beliefs about the state of your life and story.

If you believe you are a bad provider, it would be no surprise that you would cast a spouse or significant other who reminds you regularly that this is the case.

If you believe you are not a leader, you will find yourself in a partnership, suffering an abusive alpha partner who never acknowledges your value or contribution, and never misses an opportunity to subordinate you in front of others.

The same phenomena can emerge from the context within which you place yourself. If you believe you are a lousy salesman, you may well find yourself working in a used car dealership on the front lines, with the lowest sales record in the history of the dealership.

If you feel socially awkward and uncomfortable dealing with people, you can find yourself working as a customer service representative, providing unceasing opportunity for confirming that discomfort.

The key question is whether you recognize that your decisions and their consequences are not being driven by undistorted motivations.

They are driven by a hidden goal, which is to confirm a negative core belief.

> *Once the negative driver is removed, you are both entitled and enabled to clean house, recast the musical, rewrite the book, and create a new story reflective of your authentic dreams and desires.*

The last piece of the fake news puzzle is your fine-tuned selectivity when it comes to evidence gathering in support of your hidden goals.

We are surrounded by a plethora of signals via multimedia advertising and entertainment, calculated to project images of an ideal, whether in physical appearance, affluence, age, lifestyle, sensuality, or taste.

The effect of this messaging is to feed negative self-judgment and self-image. The decision is: do you choose to devote time and attention to these signals, and subject yourself to their influence and effects, or not?

If the negative self-judgment is transcended, then the driver to seek out and absorb non-self-affirming signals is removed. This frees you to make choices about changing whatever might have previously been the basis for your discontent.

So if you long for the days of being slimmer, shifting to exercising rather than watching perfect bodies on TV while eating junk food might be a way to change your physique, health and wellbeing.

Consciousness and Intentionality

When taking on where to go or what to do next, you may be tempted to focus on a single goal as the first step toward salvation.

Although seemingly logical, focusing on a single goal can tend to bias the choices available regarding how to get there. Following a straight line from point A to point B may not be the best approach.

We know it is a cliché; however, your greatest satisfaction and joy can actually be in the journey taken, and what is experienced along the way.

The post-PA mindset loves goal-oriented constructions- lots of room for narrowing choices and limiting possibilities to perpetuate negative fears and beliefs.

Setting a different course is as much about one's self-awareness in the doing, as it is about what you actually choose to do. Resorting to the familiar, the routine, the tried and true is to risk remaining stuck within the post- PA comfort zone.

Stretching out of your comfort zone means digging into all dimensions of the choices you make going forward, the where, what, with whom, how and when.

The challenge is to ask whether each choice is made consciously, with true intention, from a place of self-care and self-interest.

If the above informs your choices and actions, there is no wrong goal, nor higher authority to judge the choices you make.

Discernment in Decision Making

You can be the designer and navigator of your own journey. Under PA influences, large parts of one's discretionary life tend to be based on reflexive decisions. Reasserting conscious discernment in decision-making is key to transcending post-PA effects.

It can be extremely easy and appealing to resort to prescriptions, programs, practices, or third-party offerings as plug-and-play solutions, purporting to provide all the answers to all of one's questions or needs.

Under post-PA influence and filters, the allure of these offerings can be almost irresistible, in the face of the underlying pain and frustration infusing one's day-to- day existence.

Freed of the post-PA filters, with fully functioning discernment and self-awareness operating, it becomes possible to take ownership of the evaluation process on whether or not to adopt any one particular practice or set of tools.

Deciding whether to build or buy, to develop one's own path, protocols and approaches, or plug-and-play of others, lies at the heart of answering the "how" does one gets going.

There can be several speed bumps to watch out for when starting the evaluation process.

The first is, "If it's too good to be true, it probably is not real." There is no pot of gold at the end of a rainbow; and fairies do not dance on the head of a pin.

Any programmatic approach to how you tackle the transformation of your life must be grounded in earnest effort. No meaningful change can occur without your commitment of significant time, attention, and energy. There are no free rides or shortcuts.

The odds of a lottery ticket being a winner defy any rational basis for buying one, but the size of the payout makes purchasing a ticket irresistible.

Offers of rewards that appear to require next to no investment of time or effort hide the actual effort, work, and commitment required to achieve the promised result.

Statistics exert tremendous attraction, and can often be used to disable discernment. Generally, quantified promises of outcomes, earnings, or fantasy lifestyles are accompanied by representations of no significant demand required on your time and energy.

Numbers on their own do not equal a guarantee; and the results represented may or may not be real or achievable.

This is not to suggest that there is no value nor potential underlying these offers. It is to recognize that the power of the marketing practices employed are designed to influence, manipulate, and negate one's capacity of discernment. The sole purpose is to drive one to buy.

These practices target emotional triggers that often underlie both post-PA vulnerabilities, and the culturally programmed scarcity-as-human-condition world we live in.

The same principles, practices, and required discernment apply in the context of offerings that are targeted toward personal growth and development, spiritual awakening, mindfulness, consciousness, and religious prescriptions.

If the related engagement calls for acceptance and adherence to belief systems, submissive protocols, and unquestioning acceptance of proprietary credos (often accompanied by secret handshakes and special jargon), buyer beware.

The quid pro quo for participating can involve suspension of individual free will, sometimes accompanied by significant demands on one's time, money, and other resources.

The risk is that you can find yourself trading your own post-PA life view for a replacement plan that bears strikingly similar attributes to those that you are looking to leave behind.

The drivers and incentivization, which are usually rooted in acceptance and appreciation, are the result of manipulation of core fears and beliefs, rather than their alleviation.

87

This can also be found with hierarchical systems, where badges, certificates, titles, and rewards are an artificial meritocracy in which authority and validation are rewarded from the top.

This is not to say you cannot derive significant value and learning from them. However, approach the decision to buy with full consciousness and self-awareness of the "I" who is choosing to explore them.

It is your clarity in discernment that contextualizes the scope and nature of the commitment being made, and the benefit derived. This is central to choosing to act, not reflexively, but intentionally.

The minute you substitute the moment of choice with an externally sourced solution at the beginning of the process; it can serve as a red flag that something is amiss.

The analogy is like being a shop-a-holic, where the payoff is in the moment of acquisition, not in the pleasure of post-purchase use of the thing purchased.

There are no silver bullets. Only you can enable and execute a course of action that determines a particular outcome, as a function of your clarity regarding all of the dimensions of why you choose what you choose to do.

A variation on this can be making a sudden decision to completely change or replace a significant part of your life, with a completely new and previously unexplored alternative.

A decision to convert to a new religion, or to change professions from a credentialed field to something completely different, e.g. an accountant deciding to become a professional wrestler at the age of 65, can be a red flag for a delusional choice.

The question is whether a process of discernment is operating or not. If the decision is intrinsically impulsive, it is likely to be in service to confirmation of post-PA beliefs, including a set-up for failure.

This is not to say that you cannot decide to make a significant, even radical life change. It is not the change itself that is in question. The question is, as with all of the above examples about the "you" who is making that change, and the clarity of understanding you bring to the decision-making process.

It is more important, for achieving a post-PA transformation, that you define and own the process, choose the questions most important to ask, and bring your full cognitive, emotional, and sensorial resources to bear.

*You are the protagonist and
author of your story.
It is yours to write.*

§

LOVING THE POST-PA YOU

PA effects can involve lots of self-judgment, blame, and self-sabotage. These are internal emotional lenses. Getting over these effects involves replacing negative beliefs with a new script, as to how you feel and think about yourself on a real-time basis.

In the spirit of getting exactly what we ask for, if our post-PA beliefs have revolved around a self-critical story, it is likely our circumstances will reflect those judgments back.

This can be in the people you chose to associate with, or activities and engagements where your skills and conduct set-up others' judgments or criticisms.

If you replace all those judgments and self-imposed deficiencies with love, respect, acceptance of self, and recognition of *your* intrinsic value; you may find yourself inclined to replace or redefine the people, places, and things with which and whom you have previously surrounded yourself.

This may require asking for a new cast, attitudes, and affirmations that are self-nurturing.

It can be tricky to recognize challenges testing the "new you." These can appear in the form of people and circumstances that will attempt to reignite the old you, and the old voices that previously filled your head.

Those voices are not about the "new you;" but rather, about *their* fears and judgments of the post-PA version of you.

There is a saying, "we train people how to treat us." You may need to re-train folks around you who are part of your life, to recalibrate their way of relating to you.

Alternatively, you may need to eliminate those for whom the post-PA version of you was their primary attraction and reason for being in your life.

Living a Transcendent Life

There is no unique indicator that signals *when* you are free of the PA's effects. The experiential benefits can be incremental and ethereal.

However, the signs of transcendence to a post-PA transcendent life are embedded in the emotional experience one has on an embodied, spiritual, and intellectual basis.

How you experience the world when you open your eyes in the morning is qualitatively different when there are unlimited choices and opportunities, full awareness of your value and generative potential, and a general sense of gratitude for an abundant life.

This journey is in service to living an abundant and joyful life. It is about replacing low-level yet pervasive fear, with a profound sense of wellbeing; and a shift from defensiveness, to curiosity and excitement about what the future has in store.

It is important to maintain top-of-mind awareness about how you are doing, how far you have come, and what new is emerging. This self-monitoring affirms the underlying transformational process.

At the heart of all post-PA effects and transcendence of them, is the idea of increasing consciousness and self- awareness. Making explicit what does not serve you, or what requires change or replacement is of the essence in reawakening the greatest, grandest, and fullest version of your life.

Setting Boundaries

Under post-PA effects' influence, boundaries that define how we relate to and interact with others can often be rooted in fear, and expressed or projected reflexively. A misplaced or absent boundary is only felt through its consequences, in the form of challenging interactions with others, without awareness of the driver of those challenges.
These unconscious barriers can map to isolation, social challenges, and missed opportunities to connect or engage.

A transcendent, fully self-realized you, will have a much greater awareness of your values, likes, and dislikes, in relation to what you want and do not want, what you do, and with whom you choose to do it.

This also ties into re-connection with your power and right to ask for what you want, and to say "no" to what you don't.

Setting boundaries in a clear, explicit, and aligned way, for the world and those around you, is foundational to self-care. The clearer and more directly you can communicate your boundaries to others, the more you get exactly what you want.

Conversely, the clearer you are in defining what is not okay or of interest to you, the more likely you will not find yourself on the receiving end of an undesirable result.

Bringing Back the Joy of Living

When a PA is experienced, it tends to be a killer of joy and happiness. Its impact is dependent upon a sustained daily experience rooted in post-PA fears.

It is possible, after a long enough period of being under post-PA effects, to literally forget what it means to experience joy.

The post-PA colored glasses tend to mask the myriad opportunities and relationships within which joy can be experienced.

This unconscious blinder effect can persist well past transcendence of the internal voices that enabled it.

All around you, at any given point in time, there are unlimited opportunities to connect, relate, receive, engage, and find joy.

An important part of creating the life you want, is to commit to staying present as much as possible, fullyembodied, and open to the world and people around you, and to all opportunities to proactively connect.

We fully recognize, for the introverts amongst us, this can be a tall order. However, even the simplest act of making eye contact can be enough to catalyze connection.

You can go through the drive-thru, pay, grab that cup of coffee and move on; or, you can say hello, ask how they're doing, or pay a compliment, and offer thanks. This subtle change in your behavior can create growing relationships and connections that may enrich those moments, over time.

Ultimately, you are in control of and responsible for every aspect of your life; and, every interaction you have. How you choose to relate to those moments, on an experiential basis, determines what you generate as a result.

Some practice might be required to reawaken this dimension of your self-awareness, as it relates to what you project as you move through the world; and, to prioritize opportunities, places, activities, and people with whom to connect.

It has been well established by neuroscience that the simple act of smiling, or making eye contact, from a place of openness, can trigger a powerful reciprocal response from the person sitting across the table. If you project warmth, joy, and happiness; you will receive warmth, joy, and happiness back.

This is not to be confused with a common learned practice or behavior, like always smiling or being pleasant, which can be insincere, fear-based, or self-protective. Reflexive behaviors can be more likely indicators of a post-PA rooted pattern, and experienced as insincere or inauthentic by the receiver.

Reactivating true authentic joy of living is the greatest opportunity for celebration of self, life, and transcendence of the past.

§

CLOSING THOUGHTS

In this book, we have sought to:

- Frame what a Personal Apocalypse is,
- Unpack the contexts out of which PAs can arise,
- Outline some dimensions for self-diagnosis of whether you may or may not be suffering from post-PA effects, and
- Examine self-inquiries at a meta level, that may assist you with validating your self-evaluation.

Upon concluding that, "Yes, I am in fact suffering from post- PA effects," we have sought to identify and frame the challenges that can arise.

PAs can affect the foundational dimensions of your emotional, cognitive, and behavioral patterns. We have sought to identify strategies for transcending those effects.

Transcendence of these effects through creation of the space and time to reflect and to heal, we have sketched a process of self-inquiry, in service to providing a clean slate upon which a new life story can be written.

The second half of this book has sought to catalyze a process, through a series of inquiries. Any or all of them may provide an "aha" moment of resonance or insight.

This can assist you in freeing yourself from PA induced fears and limiting beliefs; and reveal a universe of opportunities and possibilities all around you.

By reading this book and responding to its calls to action, we believe a sense of who you are and all that you have to offer can be reawakened, revealing myriad means and ways that exist all around you to realize your greatest and grandest dreams.

We have not sought to prescribe what you should do in the face of finding yourself under the effects of a PA. You will note there are no recipes, templates, maps, canvases, or to-do lists provided.

Our sole desire is to help you transcend the fear-centered emotional overwhelm and self-judgment a PA can trigger; and to assist you in achieving an empowered and fully self-realized understanding of the life you want.

You will also note the absence of any specific case studies or hero's-journey stories of others. The risk of providing others' stories is the subliminal suggestion that, "If I do what they did, I will get what they got."

It was an intentional decision not to include these narratives; because we believe the challenges you face are personal to you, unique, and yours to solve. It is your story to write.

The heart of this book is to emphasize that you are the best suited, equipped, and qualified expert on the subject of you, to define, develop and implement your life's transformation path.

TRANSCENDING PERSONAL APOCALYPSE

Appendix

There is a vast array of offerings that can assist you with this journey.

We have included a list of books. We found these books to be invaluable for ourselves, friends, and in some cases for millions of people seeking to improve their lives. This list is by no means intended to be authoritative nor exhaustive.

Our recommendations are based solely on our own experience and research, in service to helping you sort the herd, and separate the wheat from the chaff.

As expressed previously, approach these offerings with discernment and due caution. They are not your salvation. They are resources that may assist you with your personal transformation.

List of Resources

- James Allen: *As a Man Thinketh*
- Alfred Adler: *Understanding Human Nature*
- Brené Brown: *Awakening Your Life's Purpose by Daring Greatly*
- Rhonda Byrne: *The Secret*

- Julia Cameron: *The Artist's Way: A Spiritual Path to Higher Creativity*
- Dale Carnegie: *How to Win Friends and Influence People*
- Paulo Coelho: *The Alchemist*
- Stephen R. Covey: *The 7 Habits of Highly Effective People*
- Victor Frankl: *Man's Search for Meaning*
- Clare Graves: *Spiral Dynamics*
- Dave Gray: *Liminal Thinking*
- Louise Hay: *You Can Heal Your Life*
- Dr. Shad Helmstetter: *What to Say When You Talk to Your Self*
- Harville Hendrix: *Getting the Love You Want*
- Esther Hicks and Jerry Hicks: *The Law of Attraction*
- Napoleon Hill: *Think and Grow Rich*
- Susan Jeffers: *Feel the Fear and Do It Anyway*
- C.G. Jung: *The Undiscovered Self: The Dilemma of the Individual in Modern Society*
- Robert Kiyosaki: *Rich Dad, Poor Dad*
- Randy Pausch: *The Last Lecture*
- M Scott Peck: *The Road Less Traveled*
- Robert M. Pirsig: *Zen and the Art of Motorcycle Maintenance*
- James Redfield: *The Celestine Prophecy*

- Tony Robbins: *Awaken the Giant Within*

- Don Miguel Ruiz: *The Four Agreements*

- Jonas Salzgeber: *The Little Book of Stoicism: Timeless Wisdom to Gain Resilience, Confidence, and Calmness*

- Andrian Teodoro: *The Power of Positive Energy*

- Eckhart Tolle: *A New Earth*

- Neale Donald Walsch: *Conversations with God: An Uncommon Dialogue (Bk. 1)*

- Ken Wilber: *A Theory of Everything*

- Marianne Williamson: *Tears to Triumph: Spiritual Healing for the Modern Plagues of Anxiety and Depression.*

An Invitation

We would like to extend an invitation. If you feel you would like to share with us and others what you have been or may be experiencing, and connect with others who share these challenges, please visit http://www.freeofpa.com or our Facebook group: **freeofPA**.

ABOUT THE AUTHORS

Doug Breitbart

When Doug Breitbart was a successful entrepreneur, attorney, and entertainment industry executive, the world as he knew it evaporated. He experienced his first Personal Apocalypse. It served as the catalyst for a 25-year journey of self-discovery, awakening, and reinvention as an Integral attorney, corporate consultant, coach, and instructor; and provided the foundation for his co-authorship of *Transcending Personal Apocalypse*.

Born and raised in New York City's Greenwich Village, Doug is a graduate of Columbia College and Fordham University School of Law. He has served as an attorney, corporate consultant, instructor, facilitator, coach, cultural catalyst, and provocateur at large.

Doug is a Certified Instructor of The Living Course, an Adlerian personal growth and development weekend workshop; and a Certified Instructor of INCAF's (International Network for Children and Families) Redirecting Children's Behavior, a six-week parenting practices program.

Doug lives in Bridgman, Michigan with his wife and two rescues, Huck and Leo. He is the co-founder of The Values Foundation.

Contact: doug@thevaluesfoundation.org

Fabián Szulanski

When Fabián Szulanski graduated with a civil engineering degree, immediately following graduation he experienced his first Personal Apocalypse, an economy and world devoid of gainful employment. After several rounds on the Personal Apocalypse merry-go-round; he finally found his life path and way forward. This catalyzed a transformational journey from the engineering world of measurement and calculation, to a 20-year journey into the nature of systems thinking, human behavior, and collaboration, as a teacher, consultant, facilitator and coach.

His human being-centered worldview provided the foundation for co-authoring *Transcending Personal Apocalypse,* and infuses his professional practice in the realms of strategic innovation and systems thinking.

Fabián holds a BS from the University of Buenos Aires, has pursued additional studies at the University of Bergen (Norway) and the ITBA (Instituto Tecnológico

de Buenos Aires), respectively in pursuit of a PhD in Leadership and Systemic Innovation.

Fabián was born and raised in Buenos Aires, Argentina where he currently resides with his wife. He is the co- founder of The Values Foundation.

Contact: fabian@thevaluesfoundation.org